Are You A Grumpy Old Man?

A Collection of Poetic Reflections

Dr. Dick Bridy

Dedication

Are You A Grumpy Old Man? is a tribute to all senior males experiencing the aging process and have not mastered the ability to cope with change. For seventy-seven years, I have been in a race to get somewhere, trying to please others and explore personal challenges and opportunities. In January of 2023, I authored a book of poems based on my interpretation and observations of *The Human Condition. Are You A Grumpy Old Man?* is a step forward to continue the analysis of "Irritable Male Syndrome" (a.k.a. "andropause"), depression, Alzheimer's and dementia, loneliness, isolation and other life changing medical events through the lens of poetry. While the majority of the poems address the challenges aging men face as part of their human condition, there will be humorous outtakes and timely quotes along the way. This collection of poems is dedicated to the long list of family and friends that endured the aging process with wisdom, dedication, authenticity, ingenuity, and the boundless capacity to savor life. I hope you enjoy reading this book of poetry as much as I enjoyed the inspiration and reflection to write it.

Introduction

Are you a Grumpy Old Man? The poems reflect the human conditions experienced by grumpy old men and are intended to describe "Irritable Male Syndrome" (a.k.a. "andropause") from the perspective of the aging male. Some of the poems are intended to be humorous, while others explore old-man irritability as the result of a combination of factors, some physiological, some psychological and all with high degree of respect and admiration for these long lived men. The poems will be based on observations and real-life experiences from the author's perspective.

As I started to read more about irritability and grumpiness, I found it is not normal to be irritable and grumpy. Andropause studies revealed that people 50 and older are generally happier than younger people. Their lives are more enjoyable with memories of childhood, family and experiences in their career, military service, education, sports, romance and many more. The percentage of grumpy old people is actually much lower than their younger counterparts.

If that's true, then what causes some older men perceived to become grumpy and irritable? A percentage of elderly men have not experienced the life they expected in their work or personal life. Many men do not have enough income to live comfortably in retirement, some are disabled, while others have chronic medical conditions such as hearing loss and glaucoma, conditions I have personally experienced.

Perhaps the most distressing human conditions are grief, loneliness and isolation. This can be particularly devastating for men who typically lose one or two close relatives or friends. If they outlive their wives and have no family in close proximity, it can be particularly overwhelming. For those living in nursing homes, the experience of isolation and loneliness can be profound, especially those who rarely get visitors and have no social life. People with Alzheimer's and Dementia have side effects of the condition and are prone to be grumpy and irritable. For many men, they see their mental faculties slipping away; they get angry because they cannot stop it.

Finally, the latest trend is to blame low testosterone (a.k.a. "Low T"), for their impatience, sarcastic attitude, grumpiness and argumentative persona. After analysis of the literature and numerous field studies, my conclusion falls into the category of chronic health problems being a bigger factor. An obese older man becomes irritable not because of low T – but because his beer belly is making his back hurt and his GERD (Acid reflux) keeps him up at night.

Please join me in this short poetic journey through the life and emotions of elderhood and the human conditions experienced by grumpy old men, based on a variety of firsthand experiences and the occasional grumpy and irritable bozo in my bathroom mirror.

POEMS

AGING

Aging is a phenomenon, a trait characteristic of all living organisms. There are more than biological aspects to aging, there are social aspects of changing roles, seniority, psychological, and medical treatment involved in the direct care of the elderly. Death and dying now become an immediate concern in their human condition. These factors create an expanded perspective and enhance the sensitivity to the psychological aspects of aging.

"Aging seems to be the only available way to live a long life."

- Kitty O'Neill Collins

A Beard is the Bald Man's Hope

My best friend was bald, so he grew a beard;
Baldness with elegance, in fashion, not weird.
I look in the mirror, my hair white as snow;
Will I go bald, in time will I know.

A man shaving his head is a self-confident act;
Many admire the man, who's well groomed, that's a fact.
Some women perceive bearded men attractive as well;
I'm starting today, in time it will tell.

Physical and social dominance, self-esteem as a trait,
Old bald man there is hope, it's never too late.
The good news is, I'm alert and alive,
Get up and out, awake the young man inside.

As I Grew Old - I Grew Into Me

As I grew old, while changing so fast,
Difficult to keep pace, tried so hard to the last.
As I grew old, rewarded for telling the truth,
Frightened to lie, from birth through my youth.

As I aged, I often went astray,
Learned from each stumble along the way.
As I grew old, no one paid attention to me,
My importance and value, my goals to be.

As I grew old, I did what they told me to do,
Trust and respect were my goals to please you.
As I grew old, I had feelings and needs,
Interests, talents, and potential, to continue to please.

As I grew old, few appreciated me,
For whom I was, not who you wanted me to be.
As I grew old, trust and respect were the keys,
To experience freedom, to live like I please.

Don't Break Your Hip

Fell off my bike and fractured my hip,
Terrible news, need to cancel our trip.
My bones are weak, porous, and brittle,
The socket is cracked right down the middle.

I knew it was bad when I hit the pavement,
The prognosis is poor, it may need a replacement.
Couple this fracture with diabetes and more,
My body is failing at seventy-four.

Is this nature's way of telling me to slow down?
Wear sensible shoes, or you'll trip to the ground.
Not watching where I am putting my feet,
Look out for that curb, you'll stumble into the street.

I just read the brochure on a prosthetic hip,
Take it easy at first, be sure not to slip.
Avoid extreme speed and sudden acceleration,
If I could do that, there'd be a wild celebration.

Elderhood

Elderhood is the gift of life after childhood and adulthood,
Filled with passion and promise, but in a seasoned vessel.
The experience of aging is a gift like no other,
A time for sharing with one another.

Elders are always so willing to give,
Based on decades of love in a life fully lived.
Each day, we continue, with time growing old,
Listeners of our stories hear our legacies unfold.

If you're sick or lost in grave dark despair,
Fear not, we are here, your heart to repair.
Bring your children and grandchildren to see us with you,
We Elders are ready to cherish children too.

While children may feel we are scary and ugly,
Elders are loving, who will hug so snuggly.
We are doddering and kind and smile most ,f the time,
If we're lucky, we will make funny sentences that rhyme.

I'm Insecure

I don't have time for this,
Said the husband to his wife.
My priorities are more important,
This is mine, not your life.

I've tried this already,
It simply doesn't work.
This is just another way for you,
To think I am a jerk.

This is a stupid idea,
Everything works just fine as is,
This might work for others,
But not for me, my miss.

Can't we think of something else,
I'm not feeling this.
Whoever came up with this idea,
Is clueless about our biz.

How Do You Expect To Get Into Heaven Old Man?

I'm a Grumpy Old Woman married to a Grumpy Old Man,
He pisses and moans, so I leave him alone.
Living with him makes life crystal clear,
There is heaven for sure; there must be hell for my dear.

That Grumpy Old Man and I have been married forever,
For 50 long-years with Obsessive Compulsive Disorder.
He barks like our dog when things are out of order,
He does not lift a finger but is always barking orders.

My grumpy man laughs at himself, or that is the rumor,
He constantly brags that he's filled with good humor.
His Alzheimer's has progressed in a new way, every day,
Not remembering who or what he did just yesterday.

He complains when it rains, it's too bright in the sun,
His food is too hot or too cold for his last downhill run.
When he dies, he gets cremated, my final marital action,
A prelude for hubby, a coming attraction.

I Am Not Old or Fat

The wrinkles some call laugh lines; they just won't go away,
A shaved head is the new fashion, when my hair turned black to grey.
What do you mean, my bones don't creak, my shoes are spanking new,
My mind is sharp, I wheeze a bit, please tell me who are you?

What extra kilos are you talking about, love handles are their name,
Stop whispering and speak louder, my hearing's just the same.
My sight is fine, damn print is small, closed caption is my friend,
Reading cheaters everywhere, in the bathroom, car and bed.

I exercise each day, my walking stick by my side,
Don't need it for stability, just a prop to walk with pride.
Getting back to your fatso claim, not funny or a joke,
Someday I'll show you that you're wrong,
But today I can't, last year my scale broke.

I'm Turning Into A Silverback

The silverback is a gorilla, a grandpappy by name,
White and gray hair in his beard and his mane.
A tender old man, and defender of all,
Risking his life for things, both great and small.

The silverback is kind and tender of heart,
With so many troops, he can't tell them apart.
His harem is sacred where he is the boss,
Maintaining peace and quiet, just do not make him cross.

He's deeply misunderstood by humans on earth,
His presence manifested by his enormous girth.
Family comes first to the patriarch at large,
Until that date when he is no longer in charge.

I'm Not Fat

"I'm Not Fat" I said in front of the mirror,
"Yes you are, you blimpo, I see it from here."
My hips are a 50, my waist 46,
Not sure of my shoulders, must be at least 56.

My belly protrudes, I can't see my feet.
My arse is so large, it swallows my bicycle seat.
BMI is at 40, grotesquely obese,
Blood pressure so high, next is coronary disease.

So I'm fat, yes I'm fat. Why do you care?
So what if my buttocks sits in two chairs.
Fat men are quite funny, more love per square inch,
With dimples and flab, just ready to pinch.

Lost Youth

My undiminished love of youth, so simple and so free,
Memories were so innocent, so blessed to be me.
The unknown future stretched its hand with many hopes and dreams,
It beckoned me to become, the man that I would be.

I look back nostalgically at my bygone days of youth, with fuzzy recollection,
The path had many a twist and turn, and few signs of direction.
Wonderment and elation were met with trickery and deception,
Fortunately, I was well informed and fine-tuned my perception.

My ride of life is over, no more time, no future be,
Here I sit an old man, looking out onto the sea.
Prepared for my sunset, when death will set me free.
How blessed I am, so grateful too, to live my life of dreams.

Muscle Tension, Soreness, Fatigue

The pain that I feel in my muscles is normal to me,
Tension and fatigue, please leave, and set me free.
My flesh is on fire, I gasp for a breath,
Is this my finale, before I find my death?

A glimpse of my life pops up in my mind,
My days as a child are far behind.
These symptoms appeared a decade ago,
Addison's disease, an immense blow.

Addison's affects adrenal glands, essential for my pleasure,
The hormones control metabolism, sugar levels, and blood pressure.
Is the cancer in my adrenal benign or is it malignant?
The symptoms are worse and becoming far more significant.

The worst news of all, my immune system is killing itself,
Hormone suppressants don't work today, I cannot save myself.
Tomorrow is the surgery, the goal to destroy,
Turn my tears of sadness into tears of joy.

My Final Days

Here I sit in a nursing home, staring at nothing special,
Sometimes I'm scared of everything, my life is now so stressful.
Please just take me home I say to them, in a desperate plea,
The nurse retorts, you have no home, please don't bother me.

Wondering how to get my life back, I don't know where to go,
I called my daughter to rescue me, she just hung up the phone.
Playing the victim game they say, they know not my inner pain,
I'm trapped inside this prison; this cold world feels like freezing rain.

My own thoughts are abusing me, there seems like no escape,
Thinking of simple things to cure the pain, there must be a mistake.
Every day I sit here, watching others suffer so,
My friends are dying one by one, soon my final show.

My past was not that beautiful, but I had my daughter and a wife,
Damn you aging, you took away my life,
Dark shadows are moving in, they soon will take control,
Counting down my last days here, dear Lord, perhaps it's time to go.

Not My Age

That's not my age; it's just not true.
My heart is young; time just flew.
I'm staring at this strange old face,
And someone else is in the mirror.

My body's not in disrepair.
I've not much grey in my brown hair.
I sometimes feel a little tired,
But go for jogs when I'm inspired.

This old age thing is not for me.
Concessions given, prescriptions free.
I'll just pretend I'm in my prime.
To age too fast would be a crime.

I'm just not 60 in my head.
It's still so long till I am dead,
So please don't see me in that way.
I'm staying young, if that's OK!

The Old Fart

My kids call me an "Old Fart",
I know that it's not true.
New knees and teeth at 60,
Lasered eyes at 62.

The 'Old' part really bothers me,
I hardly think that's true.
'Fart' is a different matter,
Some say I play a tune.

Frequently, I sneeze and cough,
The shart sure makes a mess.
Good thing I wear my large Depends,
It relieves my fears and stress.

If you're young and reading this,
You laugh and snicker now but forget what's true,
Just remember that in 50 years,
This 'Old Fart" will be you.

The Smells of Old Age

When I was young, looking for female fun,
My nose was my first sensor;
The girls were decked in their finest garb,
They smelled like Dove skin cleanser.

As time progressed, the smells enticed,
To nutmeg or other spices.
Regardless of the smells that day,
They looked and smelled much nicer.

Once married, we had kids of course,
Our bundles of joy and toil.
With wet diapers came the smell of Desitin,
The diaper rash was foiled.

Midlife arrived and by my side,
My wife wore Giorgio, her favorite fragrance.
She decked the house with fresh cut flowers,
So romantic was the essence.

So here we are, in our 70s now,
New smells upon our bodies.
A Salonpas patch adorns our back,
To sooth our excess hobbies.

The Moon Phases of Life

Some days I'm the moon, a fat sphere, pants too tight,
Like the moon, I reflect the sun's brilliant light.
My moods on a journey every 28th day,
I circle the Earth, hide and seek is the game I play.

I was born 7 decades ago, all was new, life was right,
The new moon to this earth, then right waxes in white.
Waxing crescent and quarter, then gibbous too,
At 45, I am full, like the phases my life's halfway through.

As the phases mature, it flips to the left, some ills and pains,
My tolerance is pressed, my life starts to wane,
Old age is now here, life fades to the last orbit lanes,
Life's completed its orbit, when the thin crescent remains.

When I Take My Last Breath

While I sit at my desk at 76,
No retirement in sight, I seldom get sick,
So what do I do for the <u>next</u> 10 years?
So confident at 40, but now with more fears.

Time to prepare for my next stage in life,
If my spouse dies, I will have no partner – no wife.
The businesses are stable, can endure for years to come,
But if I go first, there are no peers to bravely carry on.

Prepare I must, for change will come tomorrow,
No hesitation, indecision, or ambiguity can follow.
Yes, I am scared, worried to death,
What will happen to them when I take my last breath?

ALZHEIMER'S AND DEMENTIA

Dementia is a term that is used to cover a variety of symptoms associated with declining mental ability. It is a medical condition of the brain and not specifically a psychological or mental illness, although there can be behavioral and psychological symptoms associated with dementia. As we age, most of us experience forgetfulness, memory loss, and other changes that interfere with our normal daily functions. However, when we are not able to reason, experience impaired judgment and problem solving, have lapses in visual perception and changes in personality and behavior, we quite possibly have the onset of dementia. Alzheimer's disease is a specific medical disease within the scope of dementia. Alzheimer's disease damages brain cells and causes complex brain changes.

"Alzheimer's is not about the past—the successes, the accolades, the accomplishments... Alzheimer's is about the present and the struggle, the scrappy brawl, the fight to live with a disease. It's being in the present, the relationships, the experiences, which is the core of life, the courage to live in the soul."

- Greg O'Brien, On Pluto: Inside the Mind of Alzheimer's

My Dear Wife

Where have you gone, my dear old friend?
Why did you leave or did your mind just descend?
You could have told me, you were slipping away,
On Sunday you were here, on Friday, astray.

You have always been with me, for 50 short years,
You are now leaving, my eyes filled with tears.
Your mind is now fading, your words are confused,
You can no longer dress or put on your shoes.

Please stay with me, you are my life,
You are my best friend, my partner, my wife.
I look into your eyes, but the smile does not come,
You ask, "Who are you, and where are you from?"

This cruel dementia, has robbed all your skills,
Our dreams are now gone, as we sit absent of thrills.
Is your mind still with me, or gone far away,
As I sit at your bedside as you sleep away.

Dementia, You're Disgusting

Dementia, the tsunami, sits in her regal chair,
When I was young, never knew she was there.
Now at 80, she throws her vengeance at me,
Please God, I want to return to how life use to be.

That bitch, the tsunami, her mood comes at me without a word,
The wrath cuts so deep like a samurai sword.
The surge raises higher as it reaches the shore,
She consumes my mind, that unrelenting whore.

Then the waves become calm, the queen closes her door,
The tide is so peaceful as the waves hit the shore.
My feet are now standing in the sunny warm sand,
I see the devastation of the once peaceful land.

I am broken, near death from the ravage of war,
The tsunami has won this battle once more.
She sits in her throne contemplating her homecoming,
To the azure calm waters and golden beach sand, devastation forthcoming.

Dementia, A Mental Complication

Dementia is not just one disease; it's several situations;
Alzheimer's, the most well-known, with mental complications.
Our thinking skills are in decline, cognitive abilities fail severely;
What was once a mind so sharp, not working quite so clearly.

"I want this fixed," I told my Doc, he looked at me so sad;
I'll do my best to treat you, stay with me, dear old lad.
"Don't call me Old, you SOB, I'm only seventy-six;
"Just tell me what to do and I will get this fixed".

As time went on, my days a blur, I lost my fervent gumption;
Independence gone, need help with my daily functions.
Who are these people in my house, "Get out, I say to them."
Dad, we are your family, here for you, from now until the end.

I'm Just Old and Senile

There comes a time that this man can gauge,
The end of the road is approaching with old age.
If you live long enough you start losing your hair, teeth, and sight;
Your clothes either shrink or explode when too tight.

When you're offered beer. you start refusing the gift;
To spare your bladder and frequent restroom visits.
Arthritis sets in, should I still think of sex?
One would think at 90, I would be past it.

My step is now slow, stiff and unsteady,
My fright is a fall now that I am top-heavy.
My hearing is now gone, too much rock and roll;
Marine artillery with no earplugs has taken its toll.

A young man came today, he knew my name;
We talked of the past, our lives much the same.
We shared our dreams, apprehensions and fears;
He then said, "Good Night Dad, I'll always be near."

My Train Of Thought Left The Station

"All Aboard" says my mind, but my train of thought left the station,
We were talking about something in a recent conversation.
"Where was the train going?" I ask of myself,
Should I prepare for the next stop or something else?

My mind's conductor says, "It's too hard to tell,"
When you get off for your final farewell.
This train moves too fast for my mind to bear,
By the time I get settled, I'm already there.

I sit here, lost in thoughts, looking for a revelation,
While the conductor yells loudly, "All Aboard, trains leaving the station."
Searching for my next stop in my scrambled old mind,
Better hurry up quickly, or it will leave me behind.

Recognition's the key to get off the train at the station,
Lost in thought is my challenge, as in deep meditation.
To pull the emergency brake on my train of thought,
To disembark and manage the perception I brought.

I Never Left You

My wife is my love, she has Alzheimer's today;
Talk to her daily, though she may not see;
Our unbroken bond will always be.
I watch her resting; I am always quite near;
Deep in her heart, she knows that I'm here.

I watch while she sleeps, in the bed at our home;
She hears when I speak to her, when we are alone.
She cannot understand the reason why I'm gone.
But I will never leave her, I must keep us strong.

Death will not divide us, for our love is forever;
Always in our heart, one day we will be together.
Live your life and live it full measure, don't waste a day;
I am always with you, every step of the way.

Stop With The Guilt

Please stop with guilt, yes Dad's in a rest home,
I've beaten myself up so, leave me alone.
I did not abandon my husband after 41 years,
The dementia fomented his rage and his fears.

The treatment at home continued, until the symptoms got worse,
The illness progressed, my health deteriorated, then I was depressed.
Four years of resentment, fear and remorse every day,
Time to return as his wife, my kids' mother, not his nursemaid.

He is now in a place that is safe and well-staffed that he so desperately needed,
His treatment and meds, with therapy, should last, till his time on earth is completed.
His horrid illness, Dementia or Alzheimer's by name,
God give him peace, with no one to blame.

The Long Goodbye

It started with memory loss, then strange conversations,
Alzheimer's disease took control of informal situations.
The timeline was long from beginning to end,
We prayed for you; your family and your friends.

As this heartless thing called Alzheimer's made thoughts fade away,
We watched as your thoughts got obscure with each passing day.
Those gleaming blue eyes, became vacant in time,
For the leader of men, it was so undignified.

Today we seek answers each passing day,
You are finally free from this cruel disease that took you away.
What is left are the memories of our good-hearted man,
That leader, fine doctor, husband and father where our family began.

We remember that man, the hero of many,
A compassionate man with accolades plenty.
Every night when we look up and see a bright star,
We know in our hearts, exactly where you are.

The Old Man Is a Crackpot

Yes, I'm an Old Man, a crackpot to some;
I ask for advice, do the opposite for fun.
My life, a disaster, my kids are so cruel;
I spew out my rage as I sit on my stool.

Divorced and alone on life's dirty path;
I hope every being is feeling my wrath.
Not one person brought me joy, drove my friends far away;
This miserable bastard has not much to say.

Cruel at heart and bitter breath is what others see;
My heart is a void, needing love to sustain me.
On the day that I die, no one will care;
No eulogy or remembrance or nice words to share.

Peace will come with my last dying breath;
I wasted my life being cruel until death.
The fault is all mine, there's no one to blame.
This Crackpot will pass, none will remember my name.

When My Grandpap Had Dementia

My Grandpap has dementia and is beginning to suffer,
Knows not breakfast from lunch or supper.
It is a hard time in our lives, for my Mom and our family,
His days are now numbered until he is soon free.

When I come home from school, I sit next to his bed,
I fluff up his pillows behind his stiff head.
He would get up to pee, his steps slow, stiff and heavy,
I gave him his cane, to return when he was ready.

One night the phone rang, I knew the message,
The time had come for his journey and passage.
At the very same time, the rain pounded our roof,
My heart was heavy, now broken and bruised.

It has now been a decade since Grandpap passed on,
My daydreams continue playing on the swings at the park.
A butterfly landed on my hand, sat so still,
Grandpap's in heaven, he's no longer ill.

ANDROPAUSE

Andropause refers to a generalized decline of male hormones, including testosterone and dehydroepiandrosterone in middle-aged and aging men due to aging and has physical, psychological, and sexual symptoms such as fatigue, hot flashes, depression, mood changes, anxiety, loss of memory and concentration, and decreased musculoskeletal strength, which are mainly caused by a decline in testosterone level and age. The media mischaracterizes Andropause as "Male Menopause".

"Male menopause serves many purposes. It is an …epithet shorthand for describing an uncomplimentary collection of characteristics: cantankerous, moody, tearful, without interest in sex, unsexy, excessively worried, fatigued."

– *David Rubinow, Clinical Director, National Institute of Mental Health*

The Fate of Andropause

Women endure menopause, life's change at 50;
Men do the same, some no longer frisky.
The male condition is Andropause, a terrible fate;
Manboobs, nose and ear hair, and a bald head await.

The condition brings men enormous strife;
To some it's the end of sex in their daily life.
Low T is one issue, lifestyle is another;
Stop drinking, get more sleep, and exercise are others.

Upheavals, distress, and things that seem strange;
Grumpy and snappy are part of the change.
Pot belly, mushed tushy, turkey wobble, they gain too much weight;
Join a gym, start cycling, add Ozempic before it's too late.

Grumpy Old Men Are Made

Have you ever wondered what causes Grumpy Old Men?

Where do they come from, why do they exist?

What made them so grumpy, when young they had promise;

When everything was possible, excitement, adventure with plenty for all.

Life without limits, work hard and succeed,

Get married have children, the American dream.

As time wore on, that flower turned brown,

Covid, unemployment, inflation, gas prices, a budget clamp down.

When 65 arrived, no savings to spare,

Retirement income fell short even after Medicare.

Once shiny future, now a tarnished dream,

The illusion of freedom, not what it seemed.

The Grumpy Old Man does not understand,

He played by the rules, the results not as planned.

The man served his country in one of the wars,

The ribbons and metals sit in his desk drawers.

Irritable Male Syndrome

I'm a tired old man, grown weary and angry,
My libido is shot, too tired, quite frankly.
In my 77th year, I'm moody and depressed,
This just isn't me; I must be possessed.

Just 10-years ago, I'd bike every day,
Smiling at those I saw on my way.
Today no more smiles, no waves, just confusion,
More like a dream or optical illusion.

Seldom laugh, mostly frown, as I sit on the stoop,
My head once held high is now just a droop.
I pray for the day the demons will cease,
My wish for the future is to just rest in peace.

Male Menopause

He sat on the porch and looked all around,
The realization just hit him; the familiar had gone.
Life looked so strange, not what he had pictured for the past 50 years,
The dream that he fathomed was no longer there.

The pathway of his life had changed as he wandered along,
Retracing his steps, trying to see old footprints on the ground.
He turned left at the corner, he knew that was wrong,
He chose adventure, took the path that was unsafe and too long.

He should have gone right on the safe steady path,
The mistake was obvious as he took his first step.
The mire of challenge, realization of cost,
Trepidation and fear, the potential of loss.

Thanks to My Body

Hello Body, what have I done to myself,
I hurt you so many times, both inside and out.
Thank you so much for keeping me free,
Sorry for ignoring your scream, "Listen to Me."

My face is now wrinkled, heart's vessels are hard,
It is now exhausting to work in my yard.
My BP is high, libido is low,
My walk to the bathroom, once fast, is slow.

I obsessively starved, stuffed, and scrubbed you so clean,
Felt guilty the next day and sometimes would scream.
I'm sorry for hating you when you did nothing wrong,
You are my most loyal fan, standing beside me so strong.

The Guy Who is Irritated by Everything (In Prose)

I walked my dog down our street, when my elderly neighbor shouted, "Hey, keep your dog off my lawn!"

That Grumpy Old Man was the stereotypical male that bitches about every ache, pain, syndrome and indignities that come with old age.

To make life worse, my ironclad stomach is getting delicate and I have insomnia, acid reflux, joint pain, erectile dysfunction and frequent urination. (No wonder we get so easily pissed off.)

Then there are the changes that come in our family lives and work lives.

Our identity has been tied to our children and our jobs.

Our kids leave home and we retire, what do we have left?

Well, let me tell you, the world is changing around me, and rarely to my high standards.

Aging men, in particular, succumb to the nearly irresistible temptation, to look at the world these days and find it hopelessly screwed up.

The government is on the wrong track, taxes are too high, kids have no respect, athletes are on performance-enhancing drugs, the world has gone Twitter-mad, my computer locks up, my cellphone drives me insane and everybody else's cellphone drives me even more insane.

Just thinking about all of this was getting me, yes, irritated.

With all of this evidence of decline, how can we not be grumpy?

The Harley Cowboy

My mind and body's going through a change,
Is it the male menopause or perhaps a mid-life crisis?
But I'll have fun whatever the cause,
Retired now, going to live my life so damn unrighteous.

My Harley's tuned and primed for thrills,
To roar from place to place.
Shit Howdy clothes, a cowboy shirt and shoelace tie,
My Wranglers tailored tight.
Tecovas "Johnny" Boots and red bandana are ready for the ride.

Last week, I laid the Harley down, doing stupid stuff in rain,
My system's purged, my ego hurt, will now act my age.
The fireplace lit, a Jack in hand, as I sit with my pipe and slippers,
Time to watch the NFL, dressed head-to-toe in beige.

But my wife broadcasts that her Old Fool,
Has finally learned his lesson.
The Harley's sold, the cowboy garb is packed for sale,
Along with my new Stetson.

The Shrinking Man

Last week I had my physical, it seems I've lost some height,
Hey Doc, what's up, what's the source of this recent plight?
Well Johnny, it is true that you are 3 inches shorter than before,
You have what's called male menopause and you may lose some more.

More bad news is coming, your bones will get quite fragile,
The muscles in your back and legs will shorten, you'll no longer be as agile.
What makes things worse is that your sex drive will go away,
We do have shots to help with sex, you need them before you play.

My belly's fat, my hearing's shot, my eyes are nearly blind,
I get up twice a night to pee, to fight my apnea, I sleep on my right side.
Osteoporosis and the maladies of age are now my mighty plight,
The thought of shots in Mr. Johnson, is more than fearful pride.

Walk in The Park

At 77, just short of eighty, my timeline quite a span,
I walk in the park every day, some call me the Grumpy Old Man.
People say "Hello", I respond sometimes, but mostly just ignore,
That does the trick, my peace preserved, they'll not be greeting me anymore.

I dumped my wife two decades ago, her barking was distracting,
She married our next-door neighbor, last year he sent her packing.
Last week I saw her in the store, her tone was calm and sweet,
My grunt was all I said to her, the message was complete.

I did not know an easy life, mining was my trade,
Deep in the belly of the shaft with my pickaxe and shovel blade.
Yes I'm moody all day long, silence in my friend,
My dream is to continue muted until the very end.

ANGER

Anger can be classified as constructive or destructive. It originates from the "fight" component of our "fight, flight or freeze" instinct. While the response can often be physical retaliation, it can also be calling someone out, or seeking to change a system or process to fix the wrong or prevent future wrongs. Destructive anger happens when we can manage our emotions and channel our anger into actions that improve the situation or prevent the event or actions that caused the anger from happening again. Destructive anger is usually spontaneous and expressed outwardly, like lashing out at others or storming out of a room. This type of anger expression negatively impacts our physical health by raising our blood pressure and releasing stress hormones.

"Anybody can become angry—that is easy, but to be angry with the right person and to the right degree and at the right time and for the right purpose, and in the right way—that is not within everybody's power and is not easy."

– Aristotle

His Life Turned Sour

His late life filled with anger and pain,
His hours on earth started to wane.
There was no more sunshine, just thunder and rain,
What a pitiful sight, his life turned sour.

Solving problems, his ambition,
Building a world of his creation.
His prospects so bright, now a pitiful sight,
His life turned sour.

He strolled to the beach, then swam from the shore.
Looking for answers from questions before.
His refuge, the ocean, the moon, his reflection,
Never finish what he started; his life turned sour.

He wailed and moaned, "My life's not my own."
His ego was finally stripped to the bone.
Once life filled with friends, he is now alone,
His life turned sour.

I am Screaming With Anger

I am Screaming with Anger, please God tell me why,
My gut is just retching while I sit here and cry.
After time and much pain, the rage soon subsides,
Into my deep conscious, where it decides to reside.

You betray me with age, my body on fire,
The tempest burns my psyche through flames in the pyre.
Blinded by rage, the hate I cannot damper,
My emotions explode in great fits of anger.

My blood boils with anger, my fists clutched tight,
The emotion continues late in the night.
The carnage goes dim, the wreckage remains,
My mind is not thinking, senses down the drain.

I'm On Fire Inside

Violence, war, terrorism and hatred surround me,
Refugees and immigrants just want to be free,
The world is on fire, the consequence of social insanity.
Filled with anger, aggression, and hostility.

Intolerance, racism, and the abandonment of reason,
Extremism and dysfunction is the norm in DC, it feels like treason.
Social stress and intolerance are a symptom not the cause,
The justification by some to break countless laws.

Connected to poverty, family violence, and grudges,
Who are we to sit righteously and pontificate as judges?
I'm an old man, physical and mental health not that great,
Irritability, hot temper, low impulse control, my personality trait.

Is blame out there or is it in me?
I just want to get old, please let me be.
I hate what I am, it is time for a change,
My view on life must be rearranged.

CRANKY

To get angry easily, bad-tempered or irritable; other descriptions are grumpy or impatient. Cranky is a response to stressful situations or a symptom of a mental or physical health condition. Old men are often reported to feel irritable, especially when they are tired or sick. Pain, especially chronic pain, and the resulting lack of sleep and fatigue can further exacerbate the issue. Moreover, certain prescription medications can interact with each other causing mood swings and emotional outbursts.

"I know of no more disagreeable situation than to be left feeling generally angry without anybody in particular to be angry at."

– Frank Moore Colby

Cranky Old Man

I just had a stroke, everyone's looking at me,
The doctors and nurses keep staring, but what do they see?
This scared and cranky old man looks out his faraway eyes,
They ask me questions, but I cannot reply.

"Please answer my questions," I want you to try,
The nurse, quite frustrated, when I don't reply.
They bathe and feed me, the long day to fill,
Sometimes I resist them, they say "Do what you will."

Each day I awake and shudder with dread,
The dark days are upon me, my wife is long dead.
I look at the future and what do I see?
More days of this anguish heaped heavy on me.

The time is near to join father and mother,
Two brothers and three sisters, we all loved each other.
My darling awaits me to renew the vows we promised to keep,
I see their faces down the hallway so deep.

Don't Waste Your Time

At 77 years old and not much time left,
Stop wasting my time with car warrantees and insurance requests.
I struggle to stay motivated and inspired each day,
Wasting time is robbing myself, move forward I say.

I don't waste my time looking back, I'm not going that way.
No TV, web surfing, or snoozing each day,
My life is a mess, how can I make it better?
Eat food, exercise and hang out with good people together.

Do something meaningful each day, control what you can,
Wasting time, energy, and emotion is for some other old man.
The present moment is all you ever have left,
Make a difference in this world during your last days on Earth.

Live your life not someone else's, be a good man to yourself,
Associate with people who inspire you to rise higher, the trophy on your shelf.
Every day is a new day, an opportunity to better oneself,
Live it, don't waste it, the world needs your help.

Get Out Of The Middle Of The Street

It's 6 in the morning as I drive down the street,
Here are the joggers galore, Nike sneakers on feet.
An iPod and sweatpants, T-shirt and a hood,
Barely daylight, the weather is good.

Oh Jogger, damn Jogger, get out of my way,
She sweats with much pleasure at the dawn of this day.
Watch out, I nearly hit one in the center of the street,
Get on the sidewalk, you bozo, or you'll soon be dead meat.

Now here comes the pace-line, 5 women abreast,
Busy kibitzing, in their colorful vests.
Then there is Norma, her life's possessions in her cart,
She's homeless, I wonder, how did it start?

Finally, come the dogs with their walkers in tow,
The leash in tight grip so they don't walk too slow.
With tail up high and snout down to the ground,
You instantly know that it is a hound.

Hey Mutt – Get Off My Lawn

Is this you, on the bottom of my shoe?
I'm sure you can explain his messy doo-doo.
Right here on my lawn, calling cards abound,
Has no one ever told you not to leave them lying around?

My turf should be green, not doggie-doo brown,
When you empty your arse, onto my ground.
I don't mind if you pee, it's okay when you bark,
But if you doo-doo, let it be in your yard.

Stay off my turf, you miserable mutt,
When I vacuum my lawn, all that crap just gets stuck.
Yes, I vacuum my lawn, you heard it right,
I do it on Saturdays and sometimes at night.

I'm Gonna Eat Some Worms

Now that I am 77, I get the distinct impression that nobody likes me.

I am not paranoid, but I believe everyone hates me.

In fact, some people are hell bent on hurting me and ruining my life.

First it was my children, and now it is my wife.

I honestly tried to look at a situation from the other person's perspective.

To my despair, they were right, I hate me too.

I am not paranoid, but possibly schizoid,

I believe in Sigmund Freud and have felt guilty since I was a boy.

I was so despondent that I tried to eat some worms.

Big fat juicy ones, eensie weensy squeensy ones,

Down went the first one, down went the second one,

I loved how they wiggled and they squirmed.

That night I felt like Aunt Edna when she ate the fruitcake.

I was so sick, I threw up every 5 minutes.

No more worms for me, I'd rather starve to death.

Life in My Kitchen

My fridge broke down, then the toaster died,
The microwave and Keurig just sat and cried,
The toilet is blocked and refuses to flush,
The freezer's ice cream just turned to mush.

The vacuum cleaner won't suck,
The back door is stuck.
The dishwasher coughs as though on cue.
The ceiling fan squeaks with a loud attitude.

The ice maker is frozen,
The freezer's not closing.
The blender is freaking, the contents are leaking,
My wife just stands there fanatically shrieking.

The time has now come, to end this sick pun,
Wake up old man and start today's fun.
As I crawl out of bed to the kitchen scratching my head,
First jelly and butter to adorn my rye bread.

Nasty Old Man

The feisty old man turned nasty one day,
He tried to be nice but he went astray.
The Nasty Old Man sat on his stool,
Pondering why his actions are sometimes so cruel.

He wants to be nicer at the start of each day,
But fails so miserably, as time passes away.
His life squandered, on that nasty mean path,
Why must everyone feel his wrath?

A life of not knowing, why meanness began,
Often reminded, that he was a Nasty Old Man.
When he passes, he worries that no one will care,
None of his family will have nice words to share.

So goes the saga of the Nasty Old Man,
Self-destruction on steroids, since his nasty began.
How sad it will be when he takes his last breath,
Knowing that peace won't come until death.

Shut Off Your Damned Cell Phone

"Shut off that damned cell phone," I said to the freak,
"I'm trying to read quietly; not hear you speak."
The noise is endless, on a bus, in a mall,
In a bar, in my office, or at a game of football.

You're frying your gray matter on that mobile phone,
With Bluetooth ablazing, you're never alone.
Your ears did not pop, it was brain cells instead,
Your skull is teaming with sounds in your head.

The cell phone is now an appendage of man,
That small earpiece just zapping your mind while it can.
Your brains are now fried, till the day that you die,
With no common sense, till you say goodbye.

The Original "Cranky Old Man"

The original 'Cranky Old Man' was really my wife,
She read and played solitaire well into the night.
She has a habit of picking her teeth,
It continues each night while I try to sleep.

Yes, I'm an old man now, damn nature is cruel,
She makes fun of my old age, says I'm just a fool.
My body just crumbs, the grace and vigor soon depart,
She said, now there's a stone, where I once had a heart.

I dribble my food on my shirt and my shorts,
The raisin bran gets caught in my throat when I snort.
My car keys are missing, along with my socks and shoes,
My wife just chortles, "...tell me something that's new."

The Pack Rat

My wife is a pack rat, throws nothing away,
Some call her a hoarder, in the closet they stay.
These tchotchkes she says, will be useful someday.
What are you saying, they're just in the way.

Sentimental, she says of the trash she has saved,
"It's taking up space just give it away."
When we married I tolerated the clutter all over,
Now the end has come due to say NO to the hoarder.

The dressers are full, the closets and cabinets too,
The temporary shed to its brim is so full.
Birthdays, graduations, holidays, achievements,
It's the mass of it all that causes disagreements.

After 50 years of marriage, the hoarding goes on,
But I laid down the law, when it spread to our lawn.
She said, what about you with your wine and cigars,
Four bikes are too many, they are yours, not ours.

Maybe she's right and not all her fault,
My rifles, pistols and ammo are locked in my vault,
My stuff has value, her stuff is junk,
Stuffing gift wrap away till next year in her trunk.

Why Am I Grumpy?

Why am I grumpy, my friends call it an art,
It keeps me quite happy, keeps them far apart.
Life is good as a grumpy old man,
Peace and quiet are relished as long as I can.

Sadness makes me happy, my day starts with a moan,
My wife is long gone, our kids are no longer home.
Grumpy is freedom as I sit on my throne,
The silence of solitude I'm free to the bone.

A smile is just grumpy turned upside down,
Inside I'm happy all day with my fixated frown.
Grumpy life is good, I see it that way,
Try it some time, it will brighten your day.

DISABILITY

A condition of the body or mind (impairment) that makes it more difficult for the person with the condition to do certain activities (activity limitation) and interact with the world around them (participation restrictions).

"My advice to other disabled people would be, concentrate on things your disability doesn't prevent you doing well, and don't regret the things it interferes with. Don't be disabled in spirit, as well as physically."

– *Stephen Hawking*

Asthma, You Bastard

When I was a teen, I smoked every day,
That's when I got asthma, it would not go away.
Panic, anxiety, nervousness, striking my system,
This damn disease has claimed a new victim.

It seems like a lifetime as I sit on this stool,
My health is a shambles, asthma is so cruel.
The story continued since I was a boy,
Not one doctor helped me, no respite, no joy,

As my lips quiver, tears run down my face,
This punishment is unjust, my fate, a disgrace.
I'm cruel in my heart and short in my breath,
Hoping that peace comes with my death.

My friends are now gone, no stories to share,
My life so alone, with no one to care.
As I sit by myself, just me to blame,
Asthma, you bastard, my life you did claim.

GERD – My Bed Partner

The inward battle never stops, anxiety leads to stress,
When acid reflux starts to churn and sing, aspiration is a mess.
There's nothing less enjoyable than gastric fluid flowing,
Burning throat and chest, to the bathroom I am going.

Pepto Bismol is my remedy to offset the acid flow,
While the tear ducts in my eyes begin to overflow.
The volcanic magma heaving is the next trauma in this tale,
My stomach aches, my head now hurts, I'd rather be in jail.

Heartache makes for good poetry, heartburn not so much,
My bed partner of GERD, not my first choice to clutch.
The bane of old age, aches, pain and heartburn,
GERD and hemorrhoids keep me awake while I toss and turn.

Glaucoma, You're Stealing My Sight

Glaucoma, they said, the thief of my sight,
I'm not giving up without a good fight.
The pressure too high, gray curtain my fright,
My world is now darker, my days are now night.

My retina is active, floating specks and cobwebs galore,
Straight lines now look wavy, blurred, distorted, and more.
My wit is still sharp, my mind is quite clear,
I can live with glaucoma, it's not much to bear.

Last night, I stumbled and tripped on the rug,
Did not spill one drop of my wine in the jug.
More bad news for me, my hearing is shot,
My ears don't work, no infection, nor blocked.

My life verdict is terminal, sad and unfair,
I can live with this sentence, my burden to bear.
No sight and no hearing, God's plan for me,
However, now I know how bad life can be.

FEAR

The unpleasant often strong emotion caused by anticipation or awareness of danger.

"Don't let the things you are afraid of—failure, change, adversity, the unknown—stop you from going after the things you want most. Instead, find the courage to do what scares you. Face your fears, and you'll uncover new and great opportunities. And it will feel good."

– *Bruce Lee*

Don't Call Me a Geezer

I'm a crafty Old Grandpa, multitalented, some say,
I can bike, chew gum and dance the hours away.
Some smarty pants called me a Geezer last week,
Was it the wrinkles, white hair or the trembling when I speak?

My good buddies are feeble, they're younger than me,
Brand new hips and shoulders, pacemakers and knees.
I'm still dapper and fit, with libido on fire,
But my friends look frail and mostly quite tired.

Fortunate I am, my teeth are my own,
My cane is for show, as I make my way home.
My secret is simple, stay active all day,
Take care of myself, a small price to pay.

There are days that I feel uninspired,
I get on my bike and go till I'm tired.
So please don't call me a Geezer, I'm still in my prime,
To admit to old aging is an inexcusable crime.

Emotions of Aging

Today I feel happy, not angry, sad, or confused,
Fearful for sure, well worn, old, and quite used.
This life of transition, self-care is a must,
Go to bed early and eat healthy, take time to adjust.

Spend time with my family, get outside and enjoy,
Ride your bike, race a car, or be a cowboy.
Is book #2 in my list of To Dos,
My human condition is mine to choose.

Embrace compassion and empathy, I have nothing to lose,
No room for loathing, regrets, self-help or foolish self-abuse,
If I feel like my life has been turned upside-down,
I'll call my shrink for some help, before tumbling down.

Forget What?

My mind remembers to forget the things that made me sad,
I'll never forget to remember the things that always made me glad.
Some friends of mine have proved to be fictitious and untrue,
I never forgot those special friends that stuck with me through and through.

I'm getting old with growing darkness, must hold my memories tight,
The years are fading rapidly, my friends stay in the light.
Most childhood memories have disappeared into the night,
Please stay with me until I lose my memory's sight.

My biggest fear is to forget the waves of days gone by,
The many laughs and hugs with friends with loving smiles of life.
I lived a life of no regrets, gave every day my best,
My goal's to remember everyone each day until I reach the end.

OCD – Practice Makes Perfect

I'm a Grumpy Old Marine with OCD to boot,
Practice Makes Perfect, they tell every recruit.
It seduces your behavior, self-torture - ignored,
Relentless execution, flawless result - the reward.

Repetition and ritual, kinetic energy for success,
Emotion is cold and alienating, says the compassionate humanist.
"Who gives a shit" barks the Old Marine,
Practice Makes Perfect like a fine-tuned machine.

OCD is not toxic, it is fear and compulsion to please,
Whether devotion to work, family or country, most do it with ease.
As time passes bye, Grumpy Old Marine's no longer in charge,
He feels useless, not needed, his prostate now large.

The perfectionist now faced with bad knees, hips and heart,
His world is changing around him, too old to restart.
He's sad and grouchy, says, "Leave me alone".
My friends are all dying, the Good Old Days - gone.

No job, friends, or interests, he turns into himself,
Refuses suggestions, he knows he needs help.
Whiskey his refuge, gotta tough it out and do it alone,
The Grumpy Old Marine dies sitting at home.

The Highly Insecure Person

With a sense of compassion,
I balance supportive and tough love.
Maintaining positivity and composure,
Support through comfort from above.

No excuses are good for me,
Face your fears and carry on.
An excuse is a truth to prove a claim,
Either do it or begone.

Cherish the right to be fearful,
Poke holes in their argument.
Face your fears, be content,
Excuses block accomplishment.

FORGETFULNESS

A negligent failure to remember or referred to as absent-mindedness.

"We survive until, by sheer stamina, we escape into the dim innocence

of our own adulthood and its forgetfulness."

– Katherine Dunn, Geek Love

I Can't Remember

My mind is forgetful, gets worse each day,
Names, dates and birthdays have faded away.
I walk into the pantry to get something, but what?
Then go back to bed, wondering if the back door was shut.

I wake in the morning, brush my teeth in the glass,
Put on my bifocals, turn on the shower full blast.
Now what have I done, the shower comes first,
Nope, wrong, it's the potty, I got it reversed.

My calendar and fridge have stickers galore,
I'm getting more forgetful, far more than before.
As I stand by mailbox, confused why I'm here,
Thought it was the reefer to get a cold beer.

Lost My Passport

At 76, I'm fit and well, got on the plane in Tijuana,
Costa Sur for two weeks, warm sun, good food and an occasional iguana.
I'm sitting in my seat, ready to land and get a taxi cab,
I checked inside my backpack; in my heart I felt a stab.

My Passport's gone, where can it be?
I had it when I boarded, it disappeared on me.
Looked under the seat in front and behind, waited for everyone to depart,
The crew and I were frantic, no Passport - thumped my heart.

Did I drop it in TJ, or did someone pick my pack?
Or did it fall between the seats when I put my luggage in the rack.
My Passport, Global Access Card and cash, I have no money,
It was Thursday night, that's not good, the US Consulate is closed till Monday.

Volaris filed a lost report, I cancelled a credit card,
Three days have passed, emotions high can't sleep, this is hard.
The Consulate phone goes to Voice Mail, too busy every day,
The Costa Sur concierge's Mom works there, my luck has found a way.

Completed DS 11 and 64 late last night,
One is for replacement, the other to report the loss so everything is right.
My flight to TJ is domestic, no Passport is now needed,
Please God, let US Customs takes a Passport Card and CA Driver's License so
my passage is completed.

Where Are My Keys?

I asked my wife last night, could you help me find my keys,
She sarcastically exclaimed, try your pants, the truck, and jeans.
They could be in my jacket, the gym bag or front door lock,
I'm getting old and frustrated; I have a mental block.

The house is now upside down, a black hole ate my keys,
I'm running late for my stretch class, help me find them please.
Found credit cards, my pocketknife, grandkids' socks and toys,
Could they be stuffed in the couch, I'm getting quite annoyed.

What is my wife's bra doing in our outdoor shed?
I found my missing headphones at the bottom of our bed.
What a dork I am today, the keys next to my cellphone,
After class, I hope my mind can get me safely home.

GRIEF

Grief is the anguish experienced after significant loss, usually the death of a beloved person. Grief often includes physiological distress, separation anxiety, confusion, yearning, obsessive dwelling on the past, and apprehension about the future.

"You will lose someone you can't live without, and your heart will be badly broken, and the bad news is that you never completely get over the loss of your beloved. But this is also the good news. They live forever in your broken heart that doesn't seal back up. And you come through. It's like having a broken leg that never heals perfectly—that still hurts when the weather gets cold, but you learn to dance with the limp."

– Anne Lamott

All My Friends Have Died

Today I sit here on my couch all alone,
I want to call friends, but they are all gone.
No Facebook, no text, no voice on the line,
These guys are my buddies, each one was all mine.

Each month we'd have breakfast or a lunch for sure,
In opera season, we'd get together far more.
In the old days we'd party, get drunk and carouse,
We'd get into trouble when we got too loud.

There were so may good times to count and recall,
Our secretaries would join us after our game of softball.
All my friends have died, I'm dead inside,
Miss them so much, wish they'd come alive.

I sit here alive, tears flow from my eyes,
Can hardly believe, my friends have all died.

My Best Friend Died

I did not know last Friday,
That God would call your name.
In life I loved you dearly,
In death, I do the same.

It broke my heart to lose you,
You did not go alone.
For part of me went with you,
The day that you went home.

You left me with our memories,
Your friendship, still my guide.
And though I cannot see you,
I feel you by my side.

Our friendship chain seems broken,
And little feels the same.
But all of us will join you,
Our chain will link again.

Deathbed Thanks to Mary Virginia

Mom, I don't think you will,
Ever fully understand.
How you've touched my life,
And made me who I am.

You allowed me to experience,
Something very hard to find.
Unconditional friendship that exists,
In my body, soul, and mind.

Perhaps you could never feel,
The admiration I have to give.
Or maybe you never realized,
Friendship is one element in one's will to live.

You were an amazing mother,
Without you in my life, who knows where I'd be.
Having you as my dear Mom,
Fulfills a special part of me.

Mom, My Sister's Mentor

Mom, you were Barbara's teacher,
A confidante and friend.
As buddies you share everything,
From birth until the end.

Barbara was Mom's everything,
Her daughter felt the same.
She made her feel important,
With encouragement and praise.

Mom let Barb know she loved her,
In so many different ways.
She guided her little princess,
Through the sunshine and dark days.

A legacy to mothers,
Our mother set the mold.
The same for her daughter,
Barbara's endless heart of gold.

Why Did You Die?

The time has come when you are laid to rest,

My heart hurts so that God surely took our best.

Please promise to look after me,

My time is coming next.

Right now I question what God has planned,

It's not meant to understand.

Save a spot up there for me,

As I mourn my dear old friend.

The thought of no more jokes from you brings tears to my eyes,

Your failing health and passing was not a great surprise.

Time to say I love you, the chance won't come again,

Goodbye, dear friend, I'll miss you so - until we meet again.

INDEPENDENCE

Independence is the complete freedom of influence from outside people or parties.

"Independence? That's middle-class blasphemy. We are all dependent on one another, every soul of us on earth."

– George Bernard Shaw

Abby's Memory

The doorbell rings and it's pouring rain, he stands there soaking wet,
My neighbor brings my lost dog home, my tears are all that's left.
That neighbor is my husband, my Ex to be quite clear,
I could not turn away my lost dog or this wet dog who once was dear.

My lost dog's name was Alfred, my husband's name was Tom,
When we separated, I was traumatized, his cheating seemed so wrong.
Two years have passed, you want to talk, please don't ruin this for me,
The time to talk has long passed, I'm single and now free.

My memories are precious, some good and not that bad,
For now they must stay memories, let the happy outweigh the sad.
I want you in my memories, when Alfred was our baby,
Today, I am in love with Alfred and someone known as Abby.

I Vacuum My Lawn

I vacuum my lawn, yes you heard it right,
It's my field of dreams; a conservationist's delight.
My grass is plastic, too green to be true,
The emerald of Ireland, not Boise State blue.

As my neighbors pass by, they smile, wave and chuckle,
I do the same, sucking leaves in the duffle.
Natural grass is home to nature's creations,
Crawling creatures can no longer reap their sensations.

The future we steer, our water be clear,
If we save water together, we'll have nothing to fear.
Life's too short to waste it, we all need to taste it,
It's time to care, before it dissolves into thin air.

I'm Useless – I Write Poetry

I'm 77, still working, still seeking,
Decided to write poetry while my mind is still reaching.
A biography, essay, interview, or scholarly journal is educational,
For me poetry is simply recreational.

Critics claim poetry ads nothing to the world or society,
They should pull their heads from their ass, forget the false piety.
Poetry for me is the mirror to my soul,
A diary or script, in which my life history is told.

Some poems are funny, other quite graphic,
Entertainment for some and others prophetic.
Analysis for some, epic for others,
The spectrum of topics quite often includes mothers.

Haikus, sonnets, epics, and free verse amongst others prevail,
Poetry for me, the most enjoyable tale.
Useless say some, no benefit they insist,
But where would I be if it didn't exist?

I'm Not Irritable, You're Irritable

I'm Not Irritable, I just feel angry, frustrated, and annoyed,
Sometimes I feel impatient, but not paranoid.
I am sleepless and depressed with anxiety to boot,
Could it be my thyroid, low blood sugar or just a lack of fruit?

As a man, PMS is out of the question,
But PTSD, chronic pain and bipolar are a suggestion.
Broke my back, my leg twice, and an aneurysm to boot,
Neurological damage, an option along the treacherous route.

No, it's not me that is irritable now,
It is you, your nitpicking and stupid questions beating my brow.
My wife's response was that it's "nit-picker," you fool,
You're a terrible speller, did you not go to school?

So I've consulted a 'Shrink' to evaluate me,
She said that I'm edgy, and unfriendly, but I disagree.
She asked if I drink and do drugs regularly,
My response was quite sharp, 'You are insulting me.'

The Dignity of Independence

Independence is my dignity, physical and mental well-being.
Individuality is the foundation of my personal believing.
Control has been my mantra, my feeling of achievement and self-worth.
I choose my clothes, my food and how I wear my hair on this earth.

Family, entrepreneurship, living dreams is my life's purpose,
Moderation is the enemy, full steam to the surface.
Still bike and swim, the arts my hidden obsession,
Relationships are important, but for some a concession.

Now getting up in years, my pace slowing down,
Isolation and loneliness are factors hanging around.
Hopelessness and depression are for other to bear,
Financial strains are mounting, no income to spare.

Just Leave Me Alone

Damn you, leave me alone, just go on home,

All I want is to sit here and be all alone.

I'm confused and I'm weak, you've made me cry,

Your excuses are feeble, don't believe your alibi.

Just walk out that door, I will see you no more,

Go back to your girlfriend or some other whore.

I don't care who she was or whatever you did,

My life will move on, I'll take care of the kids.

Just, just leave me alone to quietly decide,

My heart is broken, it feels like I died.

So please just let me be, that's the least you can do.

Fifteen years of marriage, this betrayal is on you.

Leave Me Alone

"Leave me alone," said the man to his wife,
This has something to do with our everyday life.
I need to cool down, let off steam, take a break,
My mancave is off limits, I need quiet for Pete's sake.

He sits in his dark room to ponder this matter,
His sanctuary is soundproof, seeking quiet not chatter.
Time to escape from all societal woes,
His medical exam says his life's near a close.

How do I tell my wife that I'm dying?
She will know right away, no use in lying.
I must tell her the truth, the facts I must give,
The cancer is terminal, I've got 3 months to live.

As I leave the room, my wife waiting outside,
She asks why I'm crying with tears in my eyes.
I hug her tightly and smell her gray hair,
Now is the time to tell her, I'll no longer be there.

Leave Me My Dignity

My goal to avoid my death for as long as I can,
And continue for a century being a very old man,
But when I die please arrange me with dignity and charm,
Respected everyone, did no one any harm.

I grew up a man with keen intellect,
My view of humanity, quite circumspect.
A man who believed in a divine human soul,
His wisdom refined now that he is old.

Leave this old man dignity, my mind is now lame,
This dear old professor, of plaudits and fame.
A scholar, a diplomat with a huge human heart;
He is soon to be gone, the beat barely a spark.

Ode of an Old Country Western Singer

Oh, Baby, can ya pass me that beer?

This old hillbilly redneck lives with no fear.

It's Friday drunk time, let's go race our trucks,

Ole Johnny Law will never catch up.

An F-150, 5.2 L V8, 4-wheel drive, lifted 8 inches high,

My man cave on wheels, my Babe by my side.

My pickup's my partner, the gun rack in sight,

Empty fried chicken basket and beer can inside.

Gotta girl named Peaches, her blue jeans painted on tight,

She's my down-home angel with a whole 'nother side.

Come pick me up, in your truck, she said, I wanna drive,

Bet I can hit a buck-ten again down I-55.

Our farm's red dirt road driveway is next on the right,

My mobile house is the one with the horse trailer outside.

I'm a hardworking cowboy, dirty t-shirt and jeans,

Love my nation, chew Red Man, I'm a tattooed disabled Marine.

Pickup Geezer

Some say I'm a geezer at 77,

Drive a RAM Laramie, feels like I'm cruising in heaven.

The interior's spotless, outside shines like the sun,

It roars like a lion, when I give it the gun.

Under the hood, a 5.7 Liter V8,

Smokin' down the road all square and straight.

It purrs just like a pussycat, when I fire it up,

395 horses a screaming, carrying this old grown-up!

This may be my last beast, not many years left,

This Ram like its old owner, gave life its best.

When I go they will sell it to some young family with kids,

To travel beaches and mountains with tents, bags and cribs.

ISOLATION

Social isolation can include staying home for lengthy periods of time, having no communication with family, acquaintances or friends, and/or willfully avoiding any contact with other humans when those opportunities do arise.

"Walking alone is not difficult but when we have walked a mile worth a thousand years with someone then coming back alone is what is difficult."

– *Faraaz Kazi*

Stop Yelling At Me

At 81, my hearing's poor, my sight is not much better,
Everyone here is yelling at me, the voices sound like clatter.
I've done nothing wrong, sitting in my bed, don't know what is the matter,
The ranting and raving are just too much, quiet would be much better.

Stop flogging me with words so cruel and hateful,
My will to live is done.
I really wish the noise would stop, but you've only just begun.
Stop nagging me, I say the truth, lying's not my game,
My heart is bleeding deep inside, I'm suffocating in pain.

No idea why I wrote these lines of suffering here,
Never experienced anything so difficult to bear.
Everyone in my family was such a gentle soul,
Perhaps it was a previous life, of which I'm unaware.

My Friend In the Rest Home

My friend is alone, in the regional rest home;
He's lonely, quite ill and feels left alone.
My friend has no choice but to stay in that place;
With fear and loneliness in an isolated space.

At times like these it's hard for him to stay bright;
Just sitting and waiting from dawn until night.
My task for today is to visit my friend,
We will go for a drive, then lunch at the end.

How much lightness and smiles can I bring to his day?
Let's find out this morning, I'm on my way.
We'll explore Mother Nature and all that she brings;
Listening to the sounds of life or the birds as they sing.

The joy tip for today is simple and easy;
Reach out to a person who's life is uneasy.
To breathe in fresh air, on this crispy fall day;
His mindset will change in a remarkable way.

The Socially Isolated Man

He sits isolated and alone, watching his phone;
No one has called him for weeks; he feels so alone.
He's a socially isolated man, separated from those of the heart;
No family near, his friends far apart, he sits in his chair until it is dark.

The spiritual bond between family and friends;
Is missing from life of this old men from now to the end.
As his days progress slowly and cause him to dread;
He battles each morning to get out of bed.

Imagine yourself a part of his dreary day;
How much lightness and smiles could you bring his way?
Send someone a note, a card or a poem;
Open your heart, bring this man to your home.

LONELINESS

A state of solitude or being alone and a state of mind. Loneliness causes people to feel empty, alone, and unwanted. People who are lonely often crave human contact, but their state of mind makes it more difficult to form connections with others.

"Sometimes you need to take a break from everyone and spend time alone to experience, appreciate, and love yourself."

– *Robert Tew*

I Talked to a Lady

I talked to a lady in my dreams yesterday,
She knew my name, my age and where I lived on that day.
She told me her sorrows, her dreams and her fears,
We talked about her family over her many years.

She reminisced about folks she had known in her life,
We talked about her children, her husband and times of great strife.
Her daughter's life so similar to mine,
How was this so, with the passage of time?

Her eyes were filled with awe and great fear,
Was her daughter just me, my dream was right here?
She looked quite bewildered, what did she feel?
Am I living a dream, is this a bit real?

In the moment we shared, sat in silence with just our thoughts,
Then we giggled, cried and laughed, my stomach tied up in knots.
In that moment my life was so rich and so full,
As I whispered, "Goodnight Mother," rest in peace beautiful.

I Used To Be Happy

When I was young, my life had no pressure,
I woke up each day and lived with much pleasure.
Then I aroused one day when I was a teen,
Somehow my happiness has been drained from me.

The oldest grandson, perfection, no surprise,
I must be flawless in my grandparent's eyes.
Once in a while with things not going so well,
In my mind I felt like was stuck in a cell.

Academics and sports were the quicksand for me,
Rigid, obedient, perfectionistic, controlling, and bossy, my profile to be.
While being the firstborn shaped me into who I am today,
That standard was too high, the pressure too great.

While our progeny basks in attention galore,
Is the standard too high while we ask for more?
As a parent and grandparent I'm sorry to say,
Our children and grandsons feel the same way.

Lonely Old Man

He is waiting to die, looking back on his life,
The lonely old man was missing his wife.
A body weak and fragile, but his mind is on track,
He is aware and determined and matter of fact.

His face old and wrinkled, his shoulders are stooped,
Just happy to eat well and to have a good poop.
Some days he just feels that nobody cares,
He sits in his recliner and endlessly stares.

The lonely old man, is now wheelchair bound,
Looking through photographs he recently found.
The time has now come, to leave this old life,
As he calls out to Clara, his departed wife.

Until We Meet Again

Today, we are here to celebrate your life,
The measure of its worth.
With every single life you touched,
While you were here on this earth.

Today we pay our last respects,
That's why we are all here.
We thank you for your friendship,
And the memories we hold so dear.

We are privileged to have known you,
We are family, not just friends.
We will carry you in spirit,
Until we meet again.

LOW TESTOSTERONE (A.K.A. "LOW T")

Testosterone is the "male" hormone responsible for the changes that occur in boys during puberty including deepening of the voice, growth of body hair, enlargement of the penis, development of muscle mass, and production of sperm. Testosterone plays an important role in adult men, specifically maintaining these biological functions and also playing a role in sexual function and libido. Testosterone levels also tend to decline with age. Men with low T are more likely than other men to report changes in sex drive or erections, fatigue, loss of muscle mass, irritability, poor sleep, and infertility.

"Women speak in estrogen and men listen in testosterone."

– Matt Groening

The Aging Male

Andropause, you are menopause in Men,

The result of natural ageing, my male friend.

The lowering of Testosterone occurs in every male,

It will occur sooner or later after the age of fifty.

It may be in the mind or natural ageing,

There may injury to the testes from kicking.

Cancer of the testes may need surgery or radiation,

Orchitis of the testes occur in mumps and other viral infections.

All these causes will reduce the production of testosterone,

Male menopause will result from the loss of male hormone.

Without male hormones your body muscles will weaken,

Your sex desire will then need to be strengthened.

Replacement of male hormones will help your body,

Your increase of libido will make sex a different story.

No more tiredness or hot flushes like the menopausal woman,

Your muscles will grow; you will feel like a new man.

Time to Defeat Grumpy Old Person Syndrome

We Old Men don't get grumpy with age,

We get a bad rap; they confuse anger with sage.

When I was a teen, we played football on our street,

We yelled and screamed with excitement as we compete.

Mrs. Barnes would come out on her porch and yell "STOP",

"I can't hear my soap opera," her neck veins ready to pop.

My Mom's brother Bill had dementia, he was nursing home bound,

He died at 95, not knowing anyone around.

Some have not had the career they expected, they regret every day,

Others are disabled, they cannot golf or swim, while others play.

Retirement is hell, just living to die,

Not the dream they envisioned when they retired.

Take me for example, my hearing and sight are not well,

My back and neck hurt, my body's going to hell.

My close friends are dead, and others not well,

Lonely, frustrated and angry; "Be happy" they say, now that's a hard sell.

Testosterone Blues

When I was young, could get any chick I choose.
That party's over, rather eat and then snooze.
No libido and zest, just feeling depressed,
I got a case of Testosterone Blues.

Testosterone and tequila seemed like gold,
Turned 75, now my world's turned cold.
My girlfriend's gone, my house been sold,
I got a case of Testosterone Blues.

Raised my sons and my daughters too,
They're all gone, have families too.
All alone in the retirement home,
Sick and tired of being alone,
I got a case of Testosterone Blues.

Uncle Sigmund Died

Libido is "… more than sex", said Freud,
It's the energy that comes from instincts.
The mind is where the pleasure lives,
At nightclubs and finer precincts.

The ego is the enemy, it limits the libido,
Reality is society's rule, put it back into your speedo.
"Sex" he said, "Do it often", was his favorite credo.
Then he died one fateful night, dressed in his tuxedo.

Carl Jung believed, sexuality started in adolescence,
A psychic energy to percolate, passion in the presence.
His final words "Let's have a really good wine tonight."
Beauty, wisdom and energy, to sooth his appetite.

REFLECTION

Greater sense of acceptance of self and of others; desire for connection and the means to create it; life experiences that help us make smart decisions; wisdom and empathy—all are available to us as we grow older. Gratitude for our families and our physical, mental and financial health can increase as we grow older and allow us to be glad to be alive.

"The way we experience the world around us is a direct reflection of the world within us."

– Gabrielle Bernstein

How Do I See Me?

As I look in the mirror, what do I see?
There is no other soul exactly like me.
There are flaws and imperfections from my head to my feet,
That bald headed, overweight, toothless Old Man is staring at me.

There is someone right here that few understand,
My future is desperate, I'm a sickly Old Man,
Fears, failures and mistakes is all that I see,
My fantasies, dreams, and successes are invisible to me.

No love and acceptance available to me,
The intensity of emotions is too exhausting to see.
The insecurities that reside deep within my soul,
The suffering immense burns an emotional hole.

My future is hopeless, once an incredible person,
On occasion, I fear judgement, an overwhelming burden,
I cower at confrontation; my response is uncertain.
Oh, what have I done to deserve this final curtain?

How Do You See Me?

What do you think when you look at me?

I'm an old man, so frail, a grumpy old man, my eyes can't see.

My skin is wrinkled, my hair is white;

My hearing is gone, my teeth come out at night.

My features are strong, my chin and nose are big;

My heritage is Irish but can no longer jig.

My cheeks are red, my voice is loud; my kindred spirit is alive and free;

But what are you thinking as you look at me?

My thoughts regress to my childhood days;

My father and mother, 2 brothers and 4 sisters oh how we did play.

As I smile with my eyes, you cannot see my heart;

It is so full of life, not ready to depart.

I sit in the rest home, with long days to fill;

The nurses bathe and feed me; I eat at their will.

Dark days are upon me, my wife is long dead;

My memories are vivid; I'm living and loving life over again,

in this old man's head.

I Am Okay With Me

Each day I live with me, thus I want to be fit to know,
My challenges are mine to overcome, and so.
As I look myself straight in the eye, overcoming each as the days go by,
No regrets today or when I face the setting sun.

When my time is done,
No self-hate for the things I have done.
No secrets to hide, my head held high, and my back erect,
My goal is to achieve meaningful self-respect.

Fame and wealth are not measures to love myself,
Degrees, plaques and trophies sit on the shelf.
No measure of the kind person I really am,
These bobbles are merely an 'I love me' sham.

There will be secrets about myself, skeletons hidden on a closet shelf,
Foolishly thinking no one else will know who cares once I go.
Conscience free, knowing what others will never see,
As my last breath is taken, I will be free.

I'm an Admirable Old Man

"I'm an Admirable Old Man" said the husband to his wife,
There are qualities I embodied in my personal and professional life.
My spouse looked at me with a smile and a laugh,
This should be a good one, let me sit and relax.

No, I'm serious about this, I am open to change,
Over the past seven decades I've become humble with age.
We've been married five decades, loyalty is profound,
There's a house over our head and our finances are sound.

Our friends and family know I finish what I start,
My accountability to others proved that I'm smart.
Resilience each day, to process the challenges I face,
Regardless of outcome, I do it with compassion and grace.

Integrity my hallmark, the truth lays within it,
My generous support for the arts and veterans with physical limits.
I am grateful for the people who invest in our projects,
Our success is theirs, profitability the object.

Kit You Are My Son

Kit, you are my Son-in-law that others may see,

The great news is that you will always be a Son to me.

To the man, who gave Kristin the two sons in her dreams,

Jake and Duke were the first prize, with smiles that just beam.

At 40-years old, you are halfway to the top,

A smart beautiful partner, two boys, career, no reason to stop.

You and Kristin are blessed with great promise, a lifetime ahead,

Take the ride to the future, but remember what this old man said.

Lead by example, with character and courage,

Inspire Jake and Duke and console when discouraged.

One more request for these American boys,

Take them upstairs when they scream and make noise.

Old King Charles and His Sons

Some called him Old Fashioned, holds tradition too long,
We must give him credit; he raised his sons to be strong.
William now heir to the throne, just as planned,
Harry chose freedom from the Royal demand.

It appears the rift between the Royal Family and Sussex's may last,
My money's on Charles to mend the quarrels of the past.
In his own words, he said it best, "... why didn't you do something about it,
Before I'm laid to rest."

Sustainability and the climate are not limited to the earth,
King Charles III will reconcile the Family before he meets death.
"I can remember ... wanting to heal and make things better."
The clock is ticking, face to face please, not in a letter.

What should I say, where do I start?
No time for history, why did we depart?
I love my sons, want them to love me,
Not long for this earth, "please forgive me."

Life's Ups and Downs

Through all the ups, all the downs,
Some will be there, some can't be found.
If they won't care as they should, so be it.
This is life in the way that I wish to see it.

You can give your all, or you can try not.
When they decide to leave, what have you got?
You build it up, then it breaks away.
This is life in the way I see it today.

Days come and go, true hearts stay close.
Without happiness, love is an imitation at most.
You haven't stayed close, it's hard to love you,
This is life in a way that is sadly true.

To leave behind such a feeble mind,
Forget it and pursue someone real.
This is my goal, and in time...
This will be life and the way that I feel.

Sitting On The Pot

It is 9:00 am and like it or not,
It is time to venture and sit on the pot.
The pot is close to my office and desk,
There are only 2 stalls, the handicapped is best.

With my tablet in hand, I venture outside,
Get my keys aligned in the lock on the side.
I'm in, thank goodness, not a second to spare,
The café mocha is working, urgent business right there.

The lights in the restroom, on a timer I'm aware,
First it's emails, then texts followed by my favorite - solitaire.
It seems just like minutes, but thirty have passed,
The lights go out, now in darkness, damn that time went so fast.

The old man reaches for the paper to wipe,
It's too far away, the damn roll is jammed tight,
Single ply keeps on breaking, 3 inches too short,
Time to use Wet Wipes, my last resort.

One Last Ballad

As I go through life I understand,
The changes that my body must endure,
And as for me, I've learned how to withstand,
My aging as I pass through every door.

It seems much less severe until I see,
My mirrored image, when with much surprise,
I see an old man staring back at me,
With weathered features framing sunken eyes.

I view attractive women with a glance,
And wonder how exciting it would be,
To foster just a short, intense romance,
But then recall what they must see in me.

I guess I had my chance to dance and fling,
While still a young man living out each day,
But now the time has come for me to sing,
One last ballad as I slip away.

RESOLUTION

The practice self-acceptance living with a sense of purpose, prioritizing friendships, learning, staying active and defining your own life path.

"Because one believes in oneself, one doesn't try to convince others.

Because one is content with oneself, one doesn't need others' approval.

Because one accepts oneself, the whole world accepts him or her."

— Lao Tzu

Bald Grandpa

We are all born bald, what's wrong with that?
Now I'm folic-ally challenged, sometimes wear a hat.
No hairspray or gel to shape and glue down,
No flying hair in the wind, just a shiny smooth crown.

My head is glabrous, slick and neat every day,
The difference is that I got mine the natural way.
Ladies just love my new egg-head style,
No brushes or combs, just wear it and smile.

As a Grandpa I have a new problem to share,
My nostrils and ears grow hair everywhere.
Hair is now growing in some very weird places,
My knuckles and back plus some wide-open spaces.

Death is Funny

"Dying is hilarious," my friend Michael said to me,
It's not morbid or sad, but pure comedy.
Let's talk about it first and you will see,
Death is quite funny, please listen to me.

First you stop breathing, then the body goes floppy,
You crap in your pants, then the rest is just sloppy.
Rigor mortis sets into a rigid stiff capsule,
The mouth flops open, you turn blue as a peacock's bright tassel.

Isolation is next, you go into a box,
No food or TV, just a suit, shoes and socks.
Then it's down in the ground, waiting for worms,
Unless you're cremated, then it's powder and urn.

If silence you want, it is silence you get,
Long silences are hilarious, your family attests.
Your loved ones think of you after your dead,
An audience for their lifetime, telling jokes that you said.

Death makes us look silly, dreams, aspirations, and desire,
If it does not pan out, it just goes up in fire.
We believe that our future finds success and love,
When it ends, it's a prank from God above.

I leave you now with humor from sadness,
The vivid and memorable and deepens our gladness.
Humor is honey to heal our grief,
We remember and laugh - in between, we still weep.

Charles III Legacy

The time has passed quickly, through years too fast,
Prince of Wales to King Charles, my Mum has just passed.
As he looked to the future with hope and strong will,
Must move with a purpose, no time to stand still.

Now the King with a Queen much history, some strife,
Time to live by my motto, "I Serve", that's my life.
As we pass through the valleys and hills of each day,
Together our nation will be built, while history is made.

Memories forged with our culture intact,
Loyal to all, we fly our Union Jack.
Hope must prevail as our dreams unveil,
The sun rises with hope, our determination prevails.

As we sit at the crossroads of today and tomorrow,
We must capture the moment and others will follow.
Volunteer we must, lift souls with impact,
The rewards will be endless, our legacy intact.

Don't Worry, I'm Happy

I sit here at 81, watching my family as they come,
They arrived to visit, looking so glum.
"Hi Grandpa" my grandson said to me,
Great to see you too, come sit on my knee.

My daughter's concern was there to see,
"Dad are you happy, it's important to me."
The smile on my face, a sign that my heart is at home,
I said, "Having you here, now I'm not alone."

This is my place to lay my old head,
The pillows are soft, as I sleep in my bed.
Don't worry, I'm happy with each breath I take,
My mission in life is to each day awake.

I smile as they leave, knowing it could be the last,
Some things I can't change; time passes so fast.
They know that I love them, they love me too,
My soul is at ease, the serenity is true.

I Used to Have Charm

Old men like me have lost our charm,
We took it all for granted.
As passions wain, despair sets in,
And beauty the seed unplanted.

Charm is beauty to enrich the world,
And fuel each other's passion.
Lost forever, that shiny self,
We took it all for granted.

How blind are we, who did not see,
The charm that shone so bright.
The beauty of the charm now gone,
Into the dark of night.

My Grandson Calls Me Fatso

My grandson called me fatso and it nearly broke my heart,
Sitting in my bed, eating ice cream in the dark.
Every day I'm at the gym, biking, sweating, in search of slim.
Fighting the endless battle that I know I can't win.

My BMI is 33, I'm not large by any means,
My shorts still fit, as do my jeans.
Every day it's on the scale,
The numbers say, I am still a whale.

In May I said, I need a change,
After 4 months of diets,
This scale of mine must be deranged,
The numbers were the same again.

No more bread and lots of greens,
No sugar or fats by any means.
I'm now much smaller, knees and back not sore,
My fingers now can touch the floor.

My Life's A Cliché

Clichés you see are sent forth each day,
Regardless of the topic at home, work or play.
Generalities the source of the clichés we use,
Some old as the hills, some a bolt from the blue.

They say if it's not broken don't fix it,
However, to improve makes us risk it.
There's no smoke without fire,
The meaning in fact is they think I'm a liar.

Some hate clichés and avoid them like the plague,
They get mad as a hornet's nest at those who use them each day.
At the bottom of my soul, my heart's full of sorrow,
I'll not use a cliché until the day after tomorrow.

Half full or half empty sits the glass on the ledge,
To establish if my psyche has a negative or positive edge.
While I dream I'll live forever, much to my dismay,
One thing I know for a fact, we will all die someday.

Nobody Wants a Fat Old Man

There's an old fat man looking out his bedroom window,
No friends, divorced, a drunk with a big black Caddie limo.
Nobody wants to speak with him or be in touch with him,
This old fat man in the window, his future is quite dim.

Nobody wants to know him, act, or look like him,
Not a single person wants to be seen with him, his life condition is so grim,
His belly flops over his belt like the cheese on a Habit burger,
Fat cheeks, 3 chins, bald head, lost teeth, need we go much further?

The fat man in that window just wants someone to love,
In his heart, he wants to please, and prays to God above.
There's lots to love but deep inside, I know his odds are slim,
He yells, "Please Lord there must be someone that likes a fat old man."

Old Age Ache

Today I woke up with an awful ache.
More candles are lit on my birthday cake.
Today is my anniversary,
Can't forget it anyway.

No use in fretting, as we get old,
Be grateful how our lifetime did unfold.
My life was good, not always great,
Indebted for long life and good health as my fate.

So here I am, one birthday more,
Enjoy it while I can.
Old Age mean's I've lived extended time,
My greatest gift was wisdom, since my life began.

Yes, we all get old with time,
Someday we'll all be dead.
Today's my day to celebrate,
Turn on the Grateful Dead.

Old Man, I Sit Here

An Old man, I sit here, retired but not free,
Asking myself, what was my life meant to be?
With tragedies and hard times, with moments filled with pain,
I stood up with courage to take on each day.

Loyalty is my anchor, to stay strong and true,
Integrity with decency, true blue, through and through.
I learned as a child to stand up on my own,
There were many times when I felt all alone.

A husband, father, grandfather, mentor and more,
Stand up for the helpless, in peacetime or war.
When some are abandoned, the world let them go,
There is one man to help them, to share heart and soul.

My duty as an anchor, so strong and true,
The man they rely on to get the team through.
Seven decades have passed, what was I meant to be?
The revelation was awareness; it is much more than me.

The End

I'm tired and sleepless, can't remember, feel weak,
The headaches are frequent, the prognosis is bleak.
There are days when I feel pinned down to the ground,
The heaviness of life pretends to be the last round.

My world is shaking, head spinning, can't make up my mind,
Nothing helps my confusion behind my closed eyes.
Feeling depressed and anxious, irritable and angry,
My mood swings and lost memory - don't get mad at me.

"Never Give Up" was the mantra of mine,
These three words are believing, but will all be fine?
I know I am dying but cannot comprehend,
What will happen when this life comes to an end?

The Facets of My Life

How many facets are there in my life?
Birth, hope, opportunity, happiness, then death after strife.
From the moment I arrived, it was an energetic stream,
My family is the best, my fulfilled life's dream.

Birth is the facet when it all began,
First grandchild, a boy, just as my parents planned.
Mom's side said, "A doctor," my Dad's "An entrepreneur,"
Little did they know I'd do both and much more.

Hope and opportunity were the words of that time,
Work hard, get a degree, everything will be fine.
Success was the target of young men in my day,
What they failed to mention were the potholes on the way.

There was a war at the time after my college stay,
No choice but the Marine Corps for 1216 days.
The highest achievement was my family in life,
While my children were my legacy, first prize was my wife.

As I sit here today, 77-years old,
The years ahead are uncertain, I'm told.
When the day comes for death, I'm fulfilled to the brim,
What more could I ask, a rewarded life, as the light becomes dim.

The Old Goat Is A Relic

"It is what it is," was Bill's favorite quote,
One word with terseness, in staccato, no joke.
Unflinching acceptance of events beyond his control,
This stoic Old Coach was now 71 years old.

Bob Kraft cut him Thursday January 11 '24,
No longer a fixture on the Pat's sideline once more.
The GOAT lived well, as he ran his life race,
With 333 wins, 6 Lombardi's at his designated pace.

He warned his team weekly, don't think far ahead,
You'll miss an opportunity and find regret instead.
The legendary sports icon, will start over again,
Bluster Bill will always be a Patriot, wherever he lands.

The Superficial Ass

Some say beauty is in the eye of the beholder,
This is profoundly true as we grow older.
Those that live in the physicality,
Cannot see farther than superficiality.

As a grumpy old man, he's a superficial ass,
Regardless of his wealth, he has no moral class.
Aiming for beauty may well be nice,
But vanity is defined as a venial vice.

Rich people, poor people are equals, some say,
If you're going to win in life, the superficial say, "Get a job that pays."
If wealth makes the superficial ass feel superior, his character's a disgrace,
When we get rid of the superficial ass, the world's a better place.

Beauty is on the inside, we know that it is true,
Like diamonds some need mining and refining to sparkle new.
The superficial ass can learn a lesson to save their shallow soul,
Transforming their personality to kindness, the superficial is no more.

We Need New Blood

You're too old Pete Carroll, we're setting you free,
Allen and Schneider, are you kidding me?
My teams always compete, individuals each one,
Human performance and potential are why our teams won.

We elevate our game to reach maximum consistency and performance,
Each man is unique, intense spirit, the results are enormous.
A passion for winning while caring for each,
We nurture strong connections and set goals within reach.

We are different than most, humanistic in our approach,
Aspiration is fundamental to my success as a coach.
The result is rigor, discipline, intense spirit of competition,
Each man on this team has a passion, no submission.

These gifted players, individuals each one,
They play as a team until their job is done.
I love my players and they also love me,
In the end, it's their soul that makes each so free.

Who Is That In The Mirror?

Who is that old man staring back at me?

That white haired and wrinkled face that simply won't leave.

This man with a character once so full of life,

If you don't believe me, just ask his wife.

Eyes looking tired from ages of struggles, are now stagnant and lost,

The memories of its youth, after the bridges he crossed.

A soul which was once so full of life,

Has now become sullen, after decades of strife.

The wages of stress, pain, anxiety and aging,

The war of living that never stops waging.

His badge of honor is not stress, pain or anxiety,

It's that old man's face in the mirror looking back so quietly.

Who Is That Stranger?

As I looked in the mirror, a stranger stared back so mean,
He looks familiar, but who could it be?
I smiled at him, but he scowled back it seemed,
Was this how others saw me?

I wondered to myself, "How could this be?"
Is the guy in the mirror serious or making fun of me?
The stranger continued to stare back at me,
No happiness or humor on his face could I see.

What I see was how others saw me,
Bitterness and anger from my head to my knees.
How did I let my youth turn into me?
From happy go lucky, to this cynic indeed.

My emotions were desperate, I needed to change,
The man in the shadows, his actions so strange.
If this is now me, I want to go back,
To those wonderful days when my life was on track.

RETIREMENT SYNDROME

To withdraw from one's position or occupation or from active working life. Severe cases of retirement syndrome can lead to depression and often suicidal thoughts. Therefore, counselling helps them re-orient their identity and responsibilities to accommodate the changing roles. An understanding family and support from old and new friends greatly facilitates this transition.

"Often when you think you're at the end of something, you're at the beginning of something else."

– *Fred Rogers*

Caffeine

Hot coffee is my morning drug, ice cream is best at night,
Sleep deprivation with coffee makes me higher than a kite.
When my system needs a shock, a wakeup call, a system clock,
Caffeine is my wonder drug; it gives me power to make me talk.

One day when on a caffeine binge, convinced that I could fly,
The tonic to get me through my day, the jolt that gets me high.
Dropped into Starbucks, 6 AM, found that heaven is right there,
Two shots, 3 pumps of chocolate, now bouncing everywhere.

Caffeine's my addiction, the elixir I crave each day,
It keeps my engine humming, during work and play.
Some say I am addicted, need caffeine to stay alive,
Nonsense I say, my goal is, to shift to overdrive.

Charm

The old man looking at his reflection in the lake,
As the ducks and the leaves drift far away.
The water serene and peaceful, like the end of his life,
Oh how he wished he was here with his charming wife.

She drifted away like the ducks and the leaves,
He sits here relaxed, tranquil, calm and at ease.
All good things in life must come to an end,
As we all drop away, "Gosh, I miss her", he said.

Her charm was a magical essence uncovered,
Compassion and kindness, my best friend and lover.
The time will soon come to unite once again,
Celestial companionship that will never end.

Gone Fishin'

I'm old and I'm tired on this beautiful day,
Time to go fishin', it's my time to play.
Sitting under this tree, never breaking a sweat,
Gathering my thoughts, before I forget.

The lake is pristine, the grass is so soft,
I'll discard the shoes, then take my socks off.
Time for the fishing pole, my trusted friend,
Then into the pond went the hook with the worm on the end.

The ducks were all quacking on the sparkling lake,
The birds in the trees surely kept me awake.
As I reeled the line in, wham, the trout hit the bait,
Carefully maneuvered to seal its fate.

What a beautiful creature, brown, silver and gold,
Time to retrieve it from the water, so cold.
Bright green eyes were so large, as they looked up at me,
No option to keep it, I just set it free.

I returned to my chair in the coolest of shade,
While the leaves in the tree played a soft serenade.
My friend leaped from the water in folly and fun,
I said goodbye my buddy, our job is now done.

King Charles III Misunderstood

Best understood, King Charles III,
From his quotes revealed in his own words,
"When people are uncertain about what is right and what is wrong."
Was James Hewitt Harry's father, and William mine all along?

Harry "little Spencer", had red blazing hair,
Diana's brother and uncles, the same frocks as Charles' heir.
The chronology of Diana and Hewitt's 5-year affair,
They met after Harry was born; the dates do not compare.

Let me give an example "…where conclusions often fail"…
Tabloids condemned me, the facts missed many a detail.
The divorce was not my choosing, that letter so mean,
No choice but to accept, the ruling of the Queen.

King Charles III's goal "… to heal and make things better."
"Ich Dien" (I serve) his motto, beneath the coronet on his sweater.
Carolus Rex, his title in Latin, life's duration is waning,
Cancer now looming, Prince William's in training.

You're Fired Coach

You're Fired Coach; are we on 'The Apprentice?'
We made the playoffs, so what did we miss?
The Cowboys fought and competed to win,
McCarthy and others will be fired to their embarrassing chagrin.

Let's start with making the right choice when you hire,
The greatest obligation to avoid having to fire.
Determine the problem is it performance or personal conduct?
Solve one issue at a time is appropriate construct.

Address the problem early, to avoid a typical trap.
Delaying your responsibilities, makes corrections no snap.
But I've done my best, said the coach to Jerry the boss,
If you fire me now, our hard work will be lost.

My termination settlement will cost more than a dime,
Please stick with me now, to help work through this difficult time.
Though seemingly personal, the rippling effect has begun.
Never forget the words 'You're Fired' affects everyone.